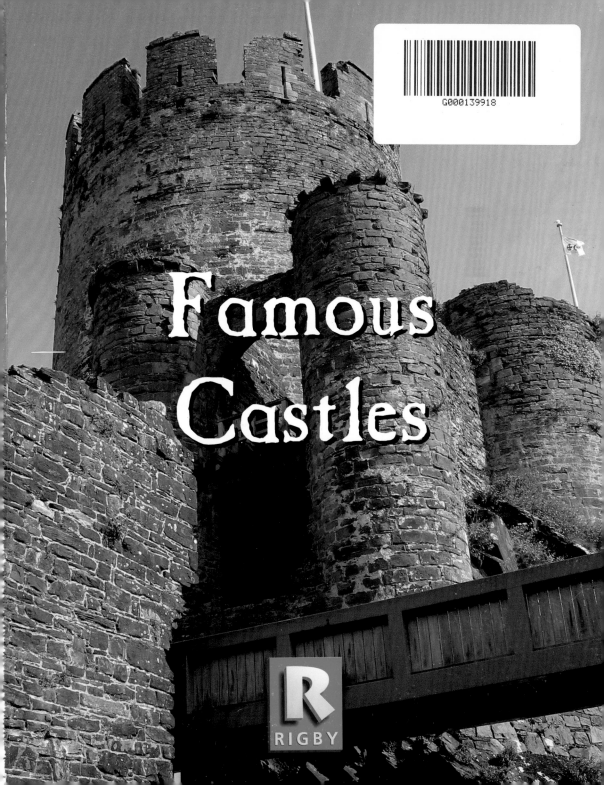

Famous Castles

RIGBY

Contents

British Castles

Windsor Castle
(say Win-zer)

Windsor Castle is the biggest castle in England. It is one of three homes used by Queen Elizabeth the 2nd.

Important people have been living in Windsor Castle for nearly one thousand years. Kings and queens have mended it, changed it and made it more comfortable.

The Round Tower

King Henry the 2nd rebuilt the Round Tower at Windsor. He knocked down the original wooden tower and rebuilt it in stone.

St George's Chapel

Edward the 4th began building St George's Chapel at Windsor Castle. It took 50 years to build and was finished by Henry the 8th.

Ten British kings and queens are buried in the chapel.

Today Windsor Castle is the largest **inhabited** castle in the world with over a *thousand* rooms! It is where the Queen stays most weekends.

The Queen also uses the castle to entertain guests from around the world. Sometimes, she holds **banquets** for her most important visitors.

The banquet table at Windsor Castle can seat 160 people!

Windsor Castle once caught fire.

FIRE FACTS

- A spotlight set a curtain on fire.

- More than 100 rooms were damaged.

- It took 15 hours to put the fire out.

- It took 5 years to restore the castle.

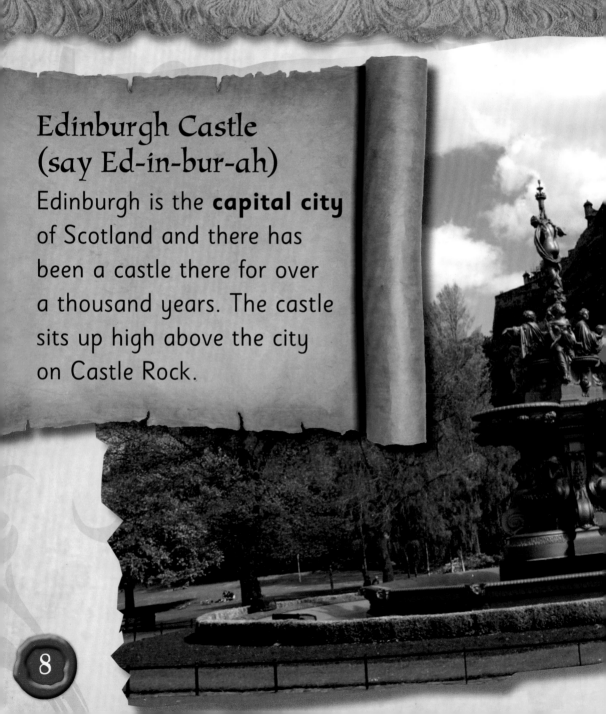

Edinburgh Castle
(say Ed-in-bur-ah)

Edinburgh is the **capital city** of Scotland and there has been a castle there for over a thousand years. The castle sits up high above the city on Castle Rock.

Over the **centuries**, Edinburgh Castle has been the home and birth place of many Scottish kings. The earliest part of the castle was built by King David the 1st. Since then the castle has been attacked and rebuilt many times.

The castle is a popular place for people to visit. About one million people a year visit it. Because the castle is so high up, visitors can see the city and the sea from the castle walls.

One of the most popular parts of the castle to visit is the Crown Room. The Scottish Crown Jewels are found here.

The One O'Clock gun is fired every day from the castle at exactly one o'clock. The sound can be heard all across the city.

Conwy Castle (say Con-way)

Conwy Castle was built by King Edward the 1st and took seven years to finish. The castle has eight towers and stands at the entrance to the River Conwy.

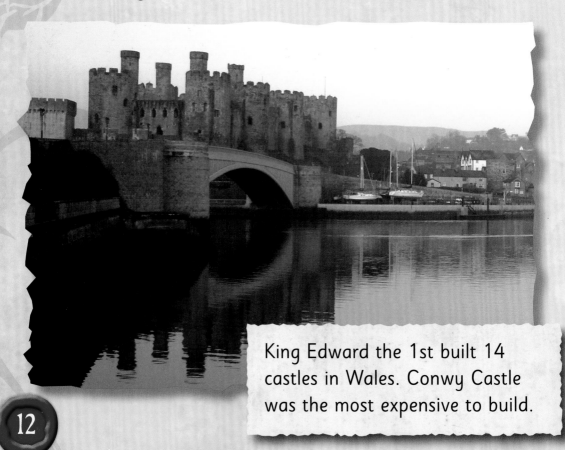

King Edward the 1st built 14 castles in Wales. Conwy Castle was the most expensive to build.

Edward also had large stone walls built around the town of Conwy to keep the people safe.

The town walls still stand today but the castle itself is empty.

Beaumaris Castle (say Bow-ma-ris)

Beaumaris was the last castle King Edward the 1st built. It was also the largest.

In the first year of building, 2,600 men worked on it. But the castle was never finished as Edward ran out of money to pay for it all!

Beaumaris Castle is a concentric castle. This means it was built in the shape of two rings, one inside the other.

The higher, inner ring of walls and towers.

The lower, outer ring of walls and towers.

The outer walls are **surrounded** by a moat.

Segovia Castle (say Se-go-vee-a)

Segovia Castle is one of the most famous and beautiful castles in Spain.

It is built high up on a rocky hill between two rivers. It is famous for its fairytale towers and blue slate roof.

The castle is almost a thousand years old and has been the home to many Spanish kings and queens.

Much of the castle was destroyed by fire, but it was restored with the help of old drawings of the castle showing how it looked before the fire.

European Castles – Germany

Sleeping Beauty's Castle

Germany is famous for its many fairytale castles – but this is the most famous of all!

This castle was built for King Ludwig the 2nd on top of the ruins of an old castle in Germany.

The castle looks like it was built long ago – even though it was only built about 130 years ago!

Ludwig's castle was the **inspiration** for Sleeping Beauty's castle at Disneyland.

This statue is in the Upper Courtyard of Ludwig's castle.

Ludwig's castle looks like an old fashioned castle from the outside. It was built high up on top of a steep hill and has high walls and tall towers.

The inside of the castle was decorated to look like an old castle, too. But Ludwig made sure his castle was built so it was warmer and more comfortable than an old castle!

European Castles – Ireland

Blarney Castle (say Blar-nee)

The ruins of Blarney Castle are in the village of Blarney, in Ireland. The castle was built by the King of Munster. It was the third castle to be built on the same site.

The **keep** at Blarney Castle is built over a cave.

Many people climb up to the top of the keep at Blarney Castle to kiss the Blarney Stone. This old stone is thought to have magical powers. It is said that everyone who kisses it will be able to talk in a charming way.

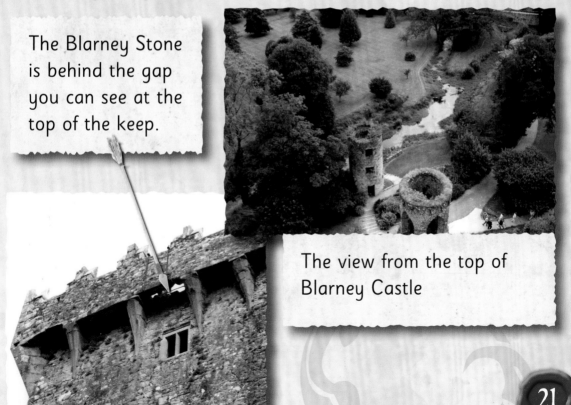

The Blarney Stone is behind the gap you can see at the top of the keep.

The view from the top of Blarney Castle

Visiting Castles

Visiting a castle can be a fun day out. Some castles hold special days when you can see things like:

- A mock battle

- Knights jousting

- A falconry display

- An archery display

The internet is a good place to search for photos and facts about the castle you want to visit.